Copyright © Nicholas
book may be reproduce
electronic or mechanical, including photocopying, recording, or by any information storage and retrieval system, without permission in writing from the publisher.

King Writing

Mount Morris, MI 48458

Chosen

Designed by Nicholas Maze

Publisher's Note: Although the author and publisher have made every effort to ensure that the information in this book was correct at press time, the author and publisher do not assume and hereby disclaim any liability to any party for any loss, damage, or disruption caused by errors or omissions, whether such errors or omissions result from negligence, accident, or any other cause.

ISBN: 9798326504838

Maze, Nicholas L., Chosen

Special Sales

These books are available at special discounts for bulk purchases. Special editions, including personalized covers, excerpts of existing books, and corporate imprints, can be created in large quantities for special needs. For more information e-mail maze.contact@yahoo.com.

John 15:16

Preface

What is it like to be chosen?

Meaning you didn't have to apply for the position, but it was given to you. Not only were you destined to fill those shoes, but it will be the most rewarding experience of your life. Being chosen by God must feel good; even as you experience the tests and trials along the way. Most people don't know they were called upon before they ever arrived on earth. Partially because their ancestors didn't do a great job of teaching them who they are and the role they play. Most children are not informed that they were chosen. God has a calling on your life and now it's up to you to mature in this calling.

You were a choice. This says it all. There was no mistake. Whether the birth was out of wedlock or unplanned, it was necessary for you to be here. The greatest example is Jesus Christ, Himself. Jesus was not only conceived out of wedlock, but Joseph had to be convinced that Mary's impregnation was spiritual, and he should not put her away (Matthew 1:19-21). This was an unordinary scenario and

Jesus was still a choice. His existence was chosen to save us all. This means your background doesn't determine whether God wants you or chose you. It's simply the way you were brought forth into the world. Your mother doesn't determine what your life will be, and your father doesn't determine what your life will be. The only thing that matters is that God chose you. He looked forward to your revealing to the world, because He had big plans for what you would become.

We fast forward in Jesus' life and we find a young man that is yet facing challenges. The Holy Bible never mentions a home that Jesus owned or lived in. It is in the eighth chapter of Matthew that Jesus confirmed it: "The foxes have holes, and the birds of the air have nests; but the Son of man hath not where to lay his head" (Matthew 8:20 KJV). With all His miraculous works shared throughout the Holy Bible, Jesus didn't have a place to lay His head and He was still chosen. He was still the Son of God. The controversy that followed and made Jesus a target amongst His own people didn't deny the fact that He was chosen. Even with all the people that have a place to call home in our present day, there are many void of knowing who they really are and why it is they were chosen.

You are a choice. You have an important and valuable role to play in God's Kingdom. God has never made a mistake. Every single person formed can be just as influential as the next. You have the ability to impact a world that is facing some of its darkest days. An opportunity to leave a lasting imprint that will bless generations to come, because you were chosen. In the Holy Bible, we learn about wives that were barren. They eagerly wanted to produce offspring for their husbands. Some were so desperate that they allowed their husband to impregnate their servants, just to give them a child. This means life is produced with purpose and God's grace. He could have prevented your mother from carrying a child, but God wanted you. You became God's choice for a plan that has existed since the beginning of time. Praise God that you were chosen.

Chosen

Nicholas L. Maze

Table of Contents

Faulty Choice 1

Come and Go 7

The Story of Joseph 13

Ancestry 19

Godward 25

Being Chosen 31

The Message 39

The Battle 45

Resources 51

Chosen's Responsibility 57

Favor 63

Handful of Meal 69

The Struggles of the Chosen 77

Chosen to Know God 83

The Body 89

The Process 95

Your Rightful Place 103

The Lord's Presence 111

Be Chosen 117

Faulty Choice

Faulty Choice

God's choice for this world comes with its own defects and challenges because we all are flawed. This isn't something you should feel ashamed about but appreciate the fact that we have a God that yet desires us. You should be following God's model and have grace for one another. Even those that don't follow His Word are simply human beings that lack understanding of why they exist. They are just as faulty as me and you, but they were also chosen. Could you imagine God wanting someone with a troubled past that lives uncivilized in our society? This is because God didn't choose the sin. God chose the real you. He chose your spirit.

Yet and still, our fleshly nature is automatically faulty, and now we can agree that we're no better than the next person. This is why God is so grand with His mercy and grace. He wants every one of us to have an opportunity to learn of Him and make the right decision. This is one of the most important reasons why we are chosen; to save the souls of the lost. The people that have got so comfortable in the ways of the world that they completely forget themselves. Instead, they live in an image and life that the world designed for them. A way of living, where the world determines what is right and what is wrong. But if God already established the laws of the land, what would be the need for new man made laws? The 'expiration date' that man placed on the Holy Bible has created a void throughout the earth. So as things only continue to get worse, many people still don't believe what was predicted in the very beginning. It didn't require scholars and scientists to discover what God has already shared with us.

Now, we continue to go downhill as a society. We continue to come up with man made solutions and man made rules. We continue to dance around the Holy Bible to find another option, hoping to eventually 'crack the code'. Truly believing we possess some special power of our own to make everything right with the world. This is what happens when you strip the knowledge of God from a world of people that was challenged to begin with. When individuals are more eager to support people creating their own sexual orientation than teaching the very Word of

Faulty Choice

God, where can His voice be heard? When does the world get the chance to experience their Creator? Like clockwork, God's presence gets smaller and smaller for each generation. We not only suffer losing all understanding, but we risk losing the only power we have to defeat evil on the planet.

We are absolutely a faulty selection for God to choose from, and He chooses us. This means we must inherit a Christ mindset and reach the same faulty individuals that simply don't understand what they are up against. They are entering a world that shares very little about God's Word and are instead developing the belief to do whatever comes to mind. There's no evidence of living Christ-like but instead burn both ends of the stick, until there's nothing left. If we are witnessing a world like this before our very eyes, what do the future generations have to look forward to? They could easily set the Holy Bibles on fire in the future and make the knowledge of God completely nonexistent in the world. This would be returning to a world that once existed before there was a Holy Bible.

Faulty Choice

Starting over again would be devastating for humanity, leading to the world feeling the wrath of God.

Come and Go

Come and Go

Most of us are born into the world to learn at least one language, get a job, work a career, and then die off. The devil is a liar. What's the best attack? Sell you a lie that you will believe. There's no such thing as a coincidence and people randomly having kids. You don't just come and go. The easiest way that the devil can ever attack you is to convince you to put your guard down. If you have no God inspired goal that affects this mortal realm and beyond, then you truly aren't investing much into anything. It is easy to invest in physical things, but these things get their value from humans. Even the currency that lands have been using for centuries is simply valuable because people say it is so. This means money can easily come and go. Your one dollar bill will never be spent like it was decades ago. It is not guaranteed to be permanent.

The same can't be said for when God chose you. You had to be permanent and exist long after the body decays. This experience is an opportunity to witness life on a physical planet. Along the way, you will come in contact with many individuals and also influence others. You will definitely come into the world and eventually die, but this experience is just a launching pad for all that God has in store. So, if 80 years of living on the planet is the highest level of achievement, then the devil has done his best work at brainwashing people to believe that nothing is beyond what we are currently witnessing. If there wasn't more to our existence, then people wouldn't still be inventing and creating. The source of God is unlimited. So long after you depart from this stage, there are still things in development.

One of the enemy's tactics is to convince you that all you need is a 30-year career and fixed retirement income, while on earth. We must remember that there once wasn't a such thing as a career or even receiving supplemental income for your latter years. Humans formed these things and made them mandatory in life. It eventually became more important to have a good job than to serve God. We blindly accept living according to the world, only to decease with nothing to show for the next stage of our existence. The biggest trick is having us believe there's nothing else to achieve, except income and a long life. You will never see otherwise because you haven't left your current state of existence. How could you possibly know that there was anything beyond death unless you were able to visit and see it for yourself? The Holy Bible.

God didn't need us to perform some magic trick to know what life truly is. He constantly held various individuals in position to document His work and message, so that we never had to question our purpose for existing. Ever since, the devil has remained a distraction from us ever learning this knowledge. The more we advance on the planet, the more distractions we have available to occupy our minds. If you calculate everything you use on a daily basis, most of the things didn't exist 100 years ago; even 50 years. This displays what the human race is up against. Things are rapidly changing. As soon as you learn to operate one invention, the next is being introduced. This is to make sure you never have the opportunity to rest your mind and focus on what is most valuable. This is also why it is easy to believe that this is it. You'll just come and go, like the latest technology and then be no more. The devil is the master of lies. Comparing the existence of mankind to a

Come and Go

limited product is distorting the truth and encouraging you to accept less for your life. The quicker the enemy can have you believe that you're worth nothing and you were simply born to die, the faster you can rot in hell for eternity.

The Story of Joseph

The Story of Joseph

Every person that wrote scripture in the Holy Bible was chosen to do so. Along with the writers, there were numerous people chosen for God's Plan. I believe one of the greatest examples, outside of Jesus Christ, is Joseph in the book of Genesis. Joseph had one of the most challenging, yet anointed callings on his life. One of the unique things we learn about Joseph is that he never asked for his purpose. God kept speaking to Joseph about his destiny. Even when his visions brought anger and hatred from his own brothers, God still kept speaking to Joseph. This displays how the calling on your life may not be receptive of everyone around you.

The challenge for Joseph was that he was immature in his wisdom. He didn't truly understand the power he possessed and the demons he was up against. He didn't know his visions would cause hate in the hearts of his brothers. They already had a chip on their shoulders about the affection that Joseph received from their father, Jacob. Regardless of how they were birthed into the world, they wanted what they felt should be equal towards all of

Jacob's children. This is the same type of feelings shared in current times. If an individual doesn't have the same gifts that God has given you, then you may experience hate or resentment for who you are. In your mind, you may feel what God has given you is a blessing for all of us. There are others that may think like 'the brothers' and question why you should be more special than them. "Why should you be the only one that God gives a coat of many colors?" This has always been one of the key reasons that many people deny the Word of God and the truth of His existence. If God was real, then none of us would have to suffer, right? For this reason, you are often picked out to be picked on.

The story of Joseph is so interesting because what he was up against had no effect whatsoever on God's ability to bless him. If anything, the commotion outside played right into the hand that was dealt for Joseph. It only made him greater in the eyes of his adversaries. And it wasn't just his brothers that Joseph had to face. Even when it seemed as if Joseph had 'made it' in life, he was yet faced with another challenge. This time, the wife of Joseph's own king had lied against him. But even this made Joseph greater than he was before. This is the most remarkable moment in his life because it displayed life for us. Don't let the setbacks be the deciding factors in your life. God still has an agenda to fulfill. Joseph was given his ending way before he became the right hand man to his king. So, he still hadn't became the ruler that God allowed him to see.

This says so much about God choosing you. How could Joseph ever reach the pinnacle of his life, if he hadn't been betrayed by his own brothers and left for dead? How could Joseph eventually become a ruler unless the wife lies and has him sent to prison to truly discover himself? The challenges and setbacks aren't the problems in your life. They are the steps along your ladder. They are the elements that complete your story. We must realize that Joseph becoming a ruler isn't what made the story. It's the fact of what he went through to get to the destination. God doesn't change as your circumstances change. God only becomes stronger in your life and make you better. God wants the one thing He has always wanted from every last person that has walked this earth, faith. Trust the process. Realize that you have a reason for your journey. The people sitting on the sidelines, let them sit. You wouldn't face the challenges unless there was a reason. How many of Jacob's other sons faced what Joseph had to go through? How many of Jacob's other sons became rulers of lands? Joseph's siblings were eventually blessed as well, but it was Joseph that God anointed to make it possible. It was Joseph that sacrificed. Appreciate the fact that God believes enough in you that you were chosen for His glory. Don't give up. It doesn't end here. Joseph's story couldn't end, until God fulfilled His promise.

Ancestry

Ancestry

One of the things that you'll find often in the Holy Bible is the ancestry of individuals. One of the reasons it is so important is not just that they know their history, but you also discover how a person got to where they are in life. Many of us in current times have lost this important wisdom. By knowing your lineage, you can discover your history and the values of your family. This is one of the strongest attacks of the enemy. If you lose your knowledge of who you are, you can lose everything. This is where the separation lies between God and mankind. Studying the Old Testament, we witness how a lot of the laws given were to be passed down, from generation to generation. An important act, such as sacrificing a lamb, wasn't just for the people of that time. They were instructed to always perform the sacrifice for generations to come.

Thanks to the Blood of Jesus, there is no longer a requirement for such sacrifices, but it has always been necessary to pass on the knowledge of Jesus. Something that our ancestors were religiously devoted to gradually slipped away, from generation to generation. Something so sacred and required for our lives and well being, eventually became an option. We somehow expected our need for the knowledge of God to change like an electric device. We may no longer have use for an eight-track player, but there will never be a moment in human existence that we will not need God. So, for God to be a choice is blasphemy to everything our ancestors fought against and sacrificed themselves for. Now, we witness a generation that argues against whether they choose to believe or not believe in God. As we passed on family recipes and aged photos, we forgot to include the most valuable information on the planet. We treated God the same way as the next generation, and this is why they are easily a reflection of ourselves. Most families didn't make the Word of God mandatory and a way of life, so the offspring don't believe that Jesus is the way for everlasting life.

There were periods of time that people were murdered for their beliefs in God. They were willing to die for our Creator and now people rarely find a Holy Bible in homes, let alone opening and reading them. Just like your ancestors, you too will become an ancestor for your family as life goes on. This means you too have a responsibility. We were never given a free pass to stop serving and uplifting God. He was never limited to a church building. By applying these limitations to God for the next generation, we invite curses and family issues into our lives that may take generations to get rid of because no one has taken authority in their families and recommitted themselves to God. When you allow God to be an option and not a necessity, the only other option is the devil. This means we are openly giving sin access to our innocent children that are birthed into the world.

This is another reason for the importance of being chosen. Someone has to come forward and stop the evil spirits that are reversing everything that our ancestors suffered for. You have a calling on your life to be the Moses for your people and free them from the enemy's stronghold. It doesn't matter what your race may be. We should care about the knowledge of God, more than we care about the cultures that were created along the way. We didn't originate with cultures. We originated as children of God. As time went on, we developed our own individual likes and dislikes, and developed cultures for an entire society of people. You will find this in the Holy Bible. They too established cultures, along with their own pagan gods, which were a result of creating their own beliefs. There will always be only one God. Man will never have the power to choose a god. God chose man. This is why we have been chosen to help the misinformed and reunite them with our God. We determine the future of our ancestry. We are the deciding factor for what will become of this world. Do we continue to distance ourselves from God and helplessly allow the majority to rule? Or do we utilize our God-given power that no army can defeat? We have purpose on this planet, which is why we had to be chosen. Be the voice for our lineage.

Godward

The title of this chapter is truly amazing. I had never heard the word used, until I began composing this book. I was familiar with forward or going towards something, but the dictionary tells us that Godward is moving towards God. It is an amazing experience when you go in God's direction. Some may question if this means moving towards heaven. In reality, God is everywhere. So, moving Godward is simply moving closer to Him, spiritually. A great example of how active God is in our everyday lives was shared in a lesson, where a teacher expressed by the very air you breathe is God in your life. But moving closer to God is about relationship. One of the things God desires most is a relationship. It's the reason He created us in His image. He had no plans for separation. God wants you to feel Him in every area of your life. Now that we're so engulfed in the world, it is necessary for us to move Godward in our lives.

One of the initial stages of getting closer to God involves the Holy Bible. The Holy Bible is where everything is. It is a perfectly crafted manual, which spiritually changes with time. It allows you to grow with God at your own pace.

This is one of the reasons the Holy Bible may initially feel like just another book. If you are working to have a relationship, then you must learn about the Lord you want to have a relationship with. It's the same as when you first started dating someone. You tried to find out as much as you could in order to determine your connection. Their likes and dislikes helped determine whether you two were compatible. In the Good Book, you will definitely learn about God's likes and dislikes. It is where we learn about the Ten Commandments. When you are intentional, just like in a human relationship, you will begin to have greater understanding, early on in your learning. Being able to create a schedule for studying the Word of God will help make reading the Holy Bible a normal habit. And the more you go Godward, the more the Holy Ghost will help you understand the Word of God.

Your biggest asset is communication. Nothing makes someone feel better than to know they have your attention. I can say this is the same in our relationship with God. He loves you regardless, but being attentive and purposely communicating takes the relationship to the next level.

While on a date in the beginning stages, we ask a lot of questions. So, one of the best ways to break the ice with God is to simply ask questions. Don't stop at just reading a chapter in Genesis. Ask God about what stood out to you in the scriptures. Let Him know that you want a better understanding of the message He gave us. From there, you can talk about yourself. Honestly, God is omniscience. This means He already knows, but the gift is wanting to welcome God into your life. You want to express your doubts and fears. You want a personal relationship that involves seeing God in everything you do. This is achieved through communication. This says that God isn't just a prayer, once a day. He truly is your Father that has all the answers.

One of the fastest ways to move towards God is adhering to His Word. We are born sinners, but God also provides the strength to resist sin. Following God's Word and laws is telling God that you want a serious relationship. You are not just testing the waters. It's similar to dating someone for a period of time and now you want more from the relationship. You want commitment. In order to go

Godward, we have to be committed. The most amazing part about a relationship with God is that He was always committed to you. We just had to realize who He is, and play catch up. The more you study His Word and the more you take time to talk with God, the more you will discover the importance of His laws and why they only exist to benefit you. That's the most powerful aspect about God's laws. They don't benefit Him. God already has everything. He simply wants His children to experience all He has to offer. In the world, the Holy Bible may feel like a bunch of rules and restrictions that keeps us away from something. In reality, it gives us the keys to a life that could never be dreamt of. The blessings are so miraculous and life-changing that your comprehension of the world and its faults is now completely different. You finally discover why it was worth the wait and necessary to go towards God.

Being Chosen

Discovering that God had purpose for me existing on this earth was life changing. At the time, I hadn't realized that God has purpose for every living person born into the world. One pastor puts it this way, God knew you before there was a satan. This means God knew you and your purpose, since the beginning of time. You were chosen before you were even thought of. It's learning that you were chosen that is the huge eye-opener. My discovery came in increments, because I had to be conditioned and prepared for such an important lesson. There is no way possible that I could have the level of understanding that I currently possess if God had showed me this in my earlier life. This includes the discovery of my gift. I discovered my interest in writing at a young age. I was a preteen that just wanted to create. Creating paragraphs and stories was my outlet. Never realizing that I would one day be fulfilling a role that would serve God.

One of the biggest reasons it takes time to learn who you are and what role you play for God is the number of changes you must experience to get there. My destiny is not praised by the world. Sharing the good news of our true God not only comes with responsibility but also challenges. When you become a part of God's Kingdom, you become a target for the devil. I first discovered my biggest battle when I began to mature in my knowledge of God. The enemy was witnessing my change and what the end result would be. The type of attack I experienced could have easily prevented some people from ever reaching their God-given gift. I was attacked in just about every area imaginable. The biggest blow was in my mental health. As an infant, I was diagnosed with epilepsy. My health condition eventually went away, and I was blessed to live a mostly normal life. Around the time that I began to invest more of my life into God is when the health issue returned.

I considered myself to still be in the infancy stages of knowing God, so I couldn't comprehend the attack. For most people, I simply had a health disorder. In reality, I was being taken down a road that would exist for the next ten years. Everything in my life changed. Everything that I thought to be normal felt like it was thrown out the window of a car, speeding down a highway. I was placed in a position where I could either ride out the journey with faith in God or simply give up because of all I was going through. Believe it or not, I gave up. I didn't give up because I was frustrated with God, but instead I gave up because I was desperate for a way to heal myself. I truly wanted to be myself, again. What I didn't understand was that I could never be who I once was, but I could still be a child of God. The challenge not only forced me to give up on a life that I had dedicated nearly twenty years to, but it brought a new view of God that I would have never witnessed if what I experienced had been any different. It was what many like to call the pruning stage. I was being pruned for my greatest experience yet.

My fight with the devil wasn't about being disliked by others or dealing with naysayers. The battle was much bigger. It was an all out spiritual war that not only went after my health, but my finances and even my relationships. It was almost as if I was being stripped of everything, only to unknowingly receive everything. Only to receive greater knowledge of God. By the time I made it to this stage of my life, I had written several books. Most of my writings had nothing to do with God, so I was definitely not working to my full capacity. There was so much more to be experienced. A lot of pastors teach on the importance of going through 'something' in order to truly know God. The importance of being chosen. Most pastors wouldn't be in the position they hold, unless they had the proof to back their message, unless they had an experience with God. As I mentioned, my destiny was determined before there was a devil. So even he could not stop what God had already put in place. It was now up to me. Do I let it all go and settle for less than what God had for me?

The greatness of God is His level of mercy, grace, and faith. Even when I got pushed into a corner that nearly jeopardized my eternity, Jesus was still fighting for me. Jesus was still leaving as many 'crumbs' as needed, in order for me to find my way back to my rightful place. The most unique part of this total experience is that we are given free will, so I could have easily ignored every sign from the Lord. I could have easily accepted defeat and never become the voice that God always knew I would be. So, God held His faith when I lost mine because I was chosen. This took me down a path that eventually birthed the writer that I am today. It gave me my 'experience' but even more, it gave me an undying faith in our true Lord. It made the words that I write that much more important. It created intimacy in my everyday walk with God. I was no longer just a faithful church member. I was a child of God. I was a man that has faced many challenging battles and now refused to deny God. I started to fill the shoes that He always had for me. The most amazing part is that the shoes were always there. God just needed me to get there. He just needed me to grow into who I was destined to be.

Being Chosen is such an important part of this book because it not only airs my laundry, but it allows me to share how important you are. It makes me think about the Apostle Paul, who was cast in jail for his beliefs in God and still would write letters of encouragement to his brothers and sisters. Even though I was brought down to some of my lowest levels, I am still the soldier that writes to encourage the reader. Encouraging you not to give up.

Being Chosen

The devil doesn't have one way he attacks. He goes after any place you may have a weakness, or you may struggle to withstand. He is ultimately going for your head, which kills the spirit. I'm writing to say I'm your fellow brother and I too have been in a spiritual battle. I too have lost many things. I too have suffered through challenges I couldn't control. I too have once given up. I too am sought after by the enemy that seeks to kill, steal, and destroy. I am you. We definitely don't live the same life, but we do have the same Father. We do have the same opponent, and I am living proof that you do win. Not only do you win while on earth, but you ultimately win for eternity. You win because you were chosen to win. God chose you, and being chosen means more than anything you'll experience on this planet. You can't lose. You are victorious. Glory to God for how great He is.

The Message

The Message

God has a message that He needs to get to you (Romans 10:17 NIV). And know this, God has no problem in getting the message to you. The problem is in us receiving the message. The message isn't a one page letter or a verbal announcement that we need to receive. It is a life-altering understanding that will change everything you ever knew about life. This is why it takes so long for most of us to ever receive this message. Even worse, a lot of people never accept the call. So, while God has built this story that can be shared for generations to come, many people never get past the first stage of even knowing that there was a message waiting for them. Do you realize the number of people that die every day, never having a relationship with God? This means millions upon millions of people are leaving this planet and never getting the gift that was promised to them. Not a job that eats up 30 years of your life, 8 hours a day, 40 hours a week. I'm talking about God's gift. It was made for you; not to be pushed on to the next person, because no one else has your personality, your dreams, your likes and dislikes, and so on. No one else is you, and many people go through life never getting the opportunity to totally use their gift. They never get their message.

One of the reasons you can experience life without ever receiving your message is because there are steps involved. There's a process. A level of maturity in order to even know you have a message. This is the most unique and powerful element of the Holy Bible. You can read the Holy Bible, every day for the rest of your life and it can still point something out to you that wasn't previously seen, each time you read it. This is how the Holy Bible can mean something different to each and every person on the face of this earth. It depends on what stage you are at in your life. You may not be ready to receive the message. You can still receive enlightenment and be guided by the message, but there will always be someone on a different level. This means it's definitely possible to have different interpretations of the Holy Bible. This is why thousands of people can be listening to the same sermon and maybe half of the people in attendance are deaf to the actual message. Most of us are not willing to invest what is necessary to get to the message. This is why the Holy Bible can be viewed

The Message

as racist, a message of hate, no longer applicable, and even a fairytale. At the same time, it is blowing the mind of a person that is just now receiving the message. One of the reasons it was created to begin with.

It is also why in the workforce you can have multiple people at different stages of their career, and everyone has a different view of a task at hand. What one person knows may have taken years to discover and be difficult for someone else to comprehend. And a lot of people may believe reading the Good Book, one-time or taking a class automatically puts them where they need to be. You could have read and taken notes, but your purpose was never about how much you read but about receiving your message. Even with my years of experience, I am still learning more about God. This is the most difficult part for some people to understand when it comes to knowing who God truly is. The Book isn't going to read to you like you might expect, because most people are not exposed to the process. They have limited knowledge and choose to give up. God never made Himself a one-dimensional God. There are areas of God that none of us know about

The Message

because we are yet growing as we speak. All in an attempt to get the message and ultimately commit to our God.

The beauty of God is that you don't have to know everything to know Him. God will always meet you where you are. It's all about us being sincere and truly desiring to be with Him. This is the value of knowing you have been chosen. It doesn't matter if you have barely opened your Bible in the past. God still has a message He wants to get to you. It comes down to doing our part and investing time in Him. God will begin to show more of Himself and provide a greater understanding of His Word, so that you can receive more of His message. This could be one of the reasons why Moses didn't start his own ministry, until he was in his eighties. It was necessary that Moses reached a level that made him receptive of God's message. And Moses still had challenging experiences during his close relationship to God. This doesn't mean that it'll take 80 years, but that this was necessary for Moses' situation and the message God had for him.

The Battle

The Battle

Always remember that you were never chosen to have a title. You were chosen for the battle.

Taking on the role to be a child of God is nothing like taking on a role with your employer. Many people chase titles in the workplace because it makes you look and feel important. It can also give you more power, while increasing your income. This role with God immediately places you on the battlefield. For a lot of people, you began to fight a war before you ever got the opportunity to realize you were called. This is because the devil also knows who you are. So, the earlier he starts, the more challenging the experience becomes. If he can hurt you before you ever have a chance to truly understand who God is, then there's a great possibility that you will never answer your calling. This is the biggest reason so many people doubt the name of Jesus. We must realize that even the so-called 'seasoned' men and women of God have their battles with doubt. They still question the future that may seem too good to be true. They still face temptation throughout their walk.

The Battle

The greatest example of living on the battlefield is Christ, Himself. It is important to understand that the devil believed he could tempt Jesus into disobeying God. One pastor gave an incredible view into this interaction recorded in the gospels. He simply said, the devil is not going to tempt you with something that you don't battle with. If he knows for a fact that you won't break, then what would there be to gain? So, as we follow Jesus, we see ourselves. Jesus is without a doubt the Son of God, but it is the flesh that satan went after by challenging Jesus to prove His might, which would have resulted in being disobedient to God. Our brothers and sisters mainly face the challenges of trusting God. The devil has been showing them many things: many false gods, many false teachings, many false promises, just to keep them in the world. So, by the time a mortal being gets to them with teachings from the Holy Bible, there are layers of beliefs that already exist within them. The world has way too much to offer them and way too many beliefs to discourage them. The battlefield: "There's no way you can tell me about an invisible god, with all the challenges I have to face. I would rather put my trust in someone I see every day before I ever place faith in someone I've never seen." If the devil is going over and beyond to occupy the minds of people in the world, imagine the attack that comes upon you.

You chose to be different. You decided to give Jesus a try. Along the way, you began witnessing some of the most unusual and challenging circumstances in your life because you are beyond the brainwashed. You chose to see for yourself. You chose to take it a step further. You chose to possibly become a problem for satan and his work in the world. This is why it is recommended that we go under leadership in ministry to guide us through these unknown experiences. We have no clue of how the devil is going to come after us, and a lot of people never knew they were under attack. This is what causes many people to not prosper in their walk with Jesus. They would rather return to what they're used to than battle in the unknown. We witness this in Exodus with the Israelites in Egypt. In this story, Moses had shown them many works of God, but their living conditions turned for the worst. This type of battle made them want to return to the norm that they originally cried to be rescued from (Exodus 14:10-12). They wanted better, but they couldn't handle the sacrifice. They couldn't trust in their true God, if it meant there would be a battle for it to manifest.

This is the type of storm that we all experience. Even God's children with more than thirty years of experience in their ministry are yet in a battle. The devil doesn't call off his demons simply because you reached a certain level. In reality, he will fight harder because those that grow in God are normally doing greater work to defeat the stronghold that the enemy has over this world. Don't believe for one moment that satan is ignoring the message I am writing for God's chosen. If I am putting forth my efforts to encourage God's people and help make them stronger, I am a problem. But the familiar verse informs us that greater is He that is in me than he that is in the world (John 4:4). All you need to remember is that God equipped you on the same day He put you out for battle. He didn't set you out on the battlefield to fend for yourself. Our problem is that it feels like we are by ourselves. Simply

The Battle

because God isn't physically seen as we experience our trying times, we feel helpless and give up. If you truly knew the amount of power you have, every attack of the enemy would result in being 'empty darts'. Artificial weapons that can only scare you. It's like the big, bad dog in your neighborhood. The bark is dangerous, but a bark can't hurt you. It's up to you to make it more than it is. As long as the gate limits its ability, you have nothing to fear. This is how we must view God, when we're in battle. Unless God plans to step off His throne, He is 'your gate', 'your wall' and you have nothing to fear. It doesn't matter what challenges you have faced in your life. The attack is limited, and God can restore double or more of anything you may have lost. The battle is guaranteed, but so is the victory. You won before it ever started. We just need to ride it out to witness the ending.

Resources

Resources

God is our source. Our source of everything. Any and everything that can be obtained or produced has to start from somewhere. God is the source of our existence. This is why I truly believe that what we physically have is called resources. They are not where it originally started. It is the repackaged version of our Source. This is why it is a resource. If we truly knew where our needs and wants are produced, we would put more focus on the Source and simply thank Him for the resource. This goes all the way to the air that we breathe. It is provided by our Source.

This means your occupation is simply supplication from God. If He decides you no longer need the current job to supply your needs, then trust and believe that your Source is infinite in ways of supplying your needs. You will receive new opportunities and the necessary resources to meet every need. Everything that exists on this earth is here today and can be gone tomorrow. Nothing on earth is permanent, and really nothing is guaranteed. The only guarantee we can always rely on is God, our Lord Jesus Christ, and the Holy Ghost. This is actually the reason you

Resources

haven't visually seen them, though they surround you every day. It is impossible to see God the same way you see the things of this world. Everything you visually witness on earth is created by men and women. Even the human beings that originated from the hand of God is reproduced from the relations between a man and woman. If it is obviously impossible for a person to create their creator, at what point do we expect to see God? This displays the beauty of God and His infinite power.

We can constantly debate on our personal views about God, but it can only go as far as what someone said. Witnessing God involves a spiritual revelation. It draws you to an area of your life where God chooses to reveal Himself. He allows you to discover your Source. Once we understand that He is our Source, we begin to revision the way we see resources. There are definitely things that we need to exist as humans; two of them being food and water. But most of these resources are first produced by another mortal being that is limited in their own nature. It's not the work they do that is most essential. It is the fact that God provides the productive environment to

Resources

generate our necessities. This world can only survive as long as God's hand and grace remain over us. This is why we should educate ourselves on the actual Source before we start investing time and energy in the resources. We are blessed to have a Father that doesn't immediately give up on us, simply because of our lack of understanding.

God actually continues to provide more ways to know Him; even if it's through how we communicate and interact with one another. All in an attempt for us to know Him. All in an attempt to have a real relationship with God. He knows our challenges and what we have to face while living on this planet. This is why God is always drawing our attention to seek Him out. Instead of judging one's beliefs about God, we should be constantly discovering God for ourselves and who we truly are. This means calling on God with the honest expectation that He will respond. Trusting that He has your best interest at heart, with the desire for you to fulfill all that He planned for your life. How can anyone doubt God, if they never gave Him an honest chance to reveal His place in their life? Many people take the problems of this world and automatically come to their conclusions about God. But they are basing their opinion of who He is on the behavior of other humans and what they have been doing since the beginning of time. People have allowed the resources to have too much influence in their lives, when the only primary factor in life is the Source.

Chosen's Responsibility

Chosen's Responsibility

Being chosen by God is only where it starts. Now, we know there is a role that must be filled. Studying the Holy Bible, you will discover a consistent story about being called upon. Those that serve God are required to develop themselves and discover what it is that God has for their life. This is your responsibility. One of the greatest examples involved Moses. Along his trail, Moses witnessed a burning bush that never got consumed by the fire (Exodus 3:2-4). The experience was so different that it held Moses' attention and drew him in. This is when God introduced Himself and birthed a new life within Moses. Even though Moses was eighty years of age, it was almost as if he was starting over again. Everything experienced with God was new to Moses. When you first learn that you are chosen, you will discover and experience situations outside of the norm. This is where you learn to commit to God and grow in your wisdom.

One of the greatest responsibilities in your journey is having faith. If everything is new to you, most of it may seem unusual. This is where you learn to control your second guessing and doubts, and totally commit to God. You develop a greater trust in God's plan than your current situation. You begin to realize that God is more real than anything you've ever experienced in your life. Because none of it would have ever taken place, if God didn't allow it. It's the work of God that shapes your life. Even the bad decisions that we've made and suffered the consequences, only occurred because God knew it wouldn't destroy us. Ultimately, our Father knew that the bad would work out for our good. God doesn't want any of His children to suffer but how do we make better decisions in life, if we never learn from the wrong decisions? The experiences eventually lead to a better future. Once we learn how active God is in our lives, we are then able to place more faith in Him. Faith is so important because it is the only way we get closer to God and unlock the many opportunities that He has planned for our lives.

Studying God's Word is also necessary for those that God chooses. Studying the Holy Bible and building faith go hand in hand. As you trust God more, you are able to find yourself in the Word of God. The scenarios, of course, won't be the same but the ways that God worked in their circumstances show how He can work on your behalf. Growing in God's Word also increases your awareness in the world. You begin to see the world in unique and meaningful ways. This simply motivates us to learn God's Word even more, which is an ongoing process. Your wisdom increases and you become more productive in your ministry. It is now easier to see what God has planned for your life and the potential you have for growing God's Kingdom. Studying the Word of God isn't just reading the Holy Bible every day, but also utilizing the many courses that have been developed just for this area in your life. I can testify that taking courses about the Holy Bible has greatly improved my knowledge of God and His Word. Along with taking courses, I am part of a small group, where we can discuss the Word of God and support one another. Most churches have groups established for this purpose. Your personal growth will always be necessary to grow in God.

Chosen's Responsibility

You will also be responsible for making a plan. The first plan in your life is God's and God's alone. This is why it is very important that we invest the necessary time and energy. Along with adhering to the Will of God, we must also establish an agenda for ourselves to complete God's Will. Realize that we already have a personal list of things to do, almost every single day. We have full and part-time jobs, businesses, family members that require our time, and even recreational activities that we enjoy. It's not about taking on another job but seriously committing to our calling. So, if we treat the call as something we will eventually get around to, then we are going about this all wrong. This is the importance of planning your mission to serve God. Scheduling time in your day to invest and grow in God. The more time you dedicate to God's Plan, the quicker it will become a natural responsibility of yours and beneficial for your walk with Jesus.

Favor

Favor

With chosen comes favor. God wouldn't choose you to fail. When we look at the life of Jesus Christ, God chose Him to ultimately be a sacrifice for our sins. Being wounded and eventually dying on the cross would look like a bad purpose, while on earth. In reality, it was the greatest purpose anyone could ever receive. Not only is Jesus' name known throughout the world in every language, but He returned to the throne beside His Father and the role as Lord over us all. Jesus will never be forgotten. People will constantly create images of what they believed Jesus looked like. Writers will continuously tell stories of His goodness and magnificence. He is our Lord. He is our everything. He is the only reason we can communicate with God. If that isn't a powerful purpose for one's life, then what is? He can never come down from His position.

This writes the perfect display of living life with purpose and having favor with our one and only God. Be excited that you were chosen. Trust and believe that God will give favor to you. There's a role that needs to be fulfilled and God definitely has the provision for your journey. Favor.

Favor

Even when I fell short of the mark, God was gracious enough to show mercy and display favor over my life. I was able to return to the purpose that my Father had set for me. I can confidently say the journey was not like I expected but that's the beauty of God. He isn't limited to how we view life. God is able to make the impossible become miraculous. It is His favor at work over our lives. So, when I returned 'home', the calling over my life was drastically modified. This meant my favor was altered as well. I was no longer writing a message for God in the same environment and scenario. The place and time were completely unknown because I needed to realize the presence of our Creator and His power.

My new experience came with its own challenges and sacrifices, so God's favor was like something I had never seen. It spoke to me in an intimate way because the challenges could have been very discouraging, but God had His own way of letting me know He was with me. He gave me the understanding that I was going to have to go through the process, but it wouldn't destroy me. As long as I understood this and remained committed, His favor would never leave. It didn't matter how extreme the circumstance became, because there was favor in my life. I love how Psalm 30:5 says, "For His anger lasts only a moment, but His favor lasts a lifetime; weeping may stay for the night, but rejoicing comes in the morning." This verse speaks profoundly about my experience and relationship with God. I know the decisions I made angered God. I believe that is why certain things in my life needed to be sacrificed. I had to be placed in an environment that would take me deeper into my knowledge of God. I view it as an atonement for the choices made in error. The magnificence of Psalm 30:5 is that though God's anger may last for a moment, His favor lasts a lifetime. How much more beautiful can that be? To know that we have a forgiving God that won't take His favor from your life. The epitome of having favor with our true God. I am beyond thankful and grateful that God never removed His favor from my life.

Psalm 30:5 also reassures you that your weeping is limited as well, and you can have faith in your joy returning. Yet, another perfect display of our wonderful Lord and His mercy and grace. This means you must realize that God's chosen are perfectly fine. We may, as they say, 'drop the ball' but we serve an incredibly forgiving God. A God that sees the real you, which is why He chose us. He saw me, when I could no longer see myself and took a turn for the worse. My flesh went towards destruction, but God's relationship is with my spirit; not my temporary, flawed flesh. So as painful as the experience may have been as I dealt with the challenges, the importance was the joy that would soon return. It may not be an overnight transition, but you only have to remember that your joy will return because of God's favor for a lifetime. This means that God could have placed favor over your life, twenty years ago and you still have it.

Favor doesn't have an expiration date. It's usually our limited mindset that removes the favor, because we gave up on a God that can't fail. We gave up on our Creator. He never gave up on us. Anything that God creates can't fail. This includes the creation of man and woman, who was blessed with free will, which led to them choosing to fall. Ultimately, God blessed us with our Lord Jesus Christ and gave us a way to never fall again. Favor. We just need to continue to build upon our faith; recognizing our part in the Kingdom and the favor it brings. It may not look squeaky clean on the outside but trust and believe that God will fulfill the purpose He has for your life. He revealed it to me in the most unusual and amazing way that I could have ever imagined. It's the only reason I'm writing this message today. It is nothing special about me. It is simply favor that comes with a lifetime agreement. If it had not been for favor, I would have still been building my place in hell. Or even worse, no longer living because of no covering over my life. Move in faith, move in love, and continue to move forward in God with the knowledge of His favor. Amen.

Handful of Meal

Study the Holy Bible and you will find a God that has never lacked anything. I truly mean anything. God is infinite in His power. So, when it came time to fight the works of iniquity, much wasn't needed. In reality, little is more. We must come to the realization of who God really is. God didn't need a hospital and educated doctors to form man. He used dirt. God used the least expected of earth to form one of His greatest works, an image of Himself. This is why we come into the world with such zeal and determination. We enter this planet in God's reflection. Our arrival in the world requires very little to achieve a lot.

This type of orchestry was also displayed with Moses. God used not only a little amount but what seemed to be the most challenged for His work. Moses was a known killer. Of course, God knew Moses had killed a man but even Moses' kind knew he was a killer. Yet, God went to work and displayed how any person can be called upon and changed to do His Will. He truly threw away every mirror in our 'house of doubt'. We could no longer look at ourselves and give up. We instead had to find God's reflection in us. A really remarkable understanding of God. Just because you might've loss doesn't mean you're not God's. And as long as you belong to Him, the world can never destroy you.

The devil set out on a mission to prove that he is greater than our God. This is why we see so much of the devil in the world. He is attempting to destroy God's creation at all costs. But the magnificence of God is that He doesn't need a parade, like the devil. God doesn't require banners and full spread ads to achieve His victory. Our God only wants a 'handful of meal' to make His point. He only wants His chosen to show His power. This was so beautifully displayed in the book of 1 Kings. In chapter seventeen, we come upon a woman that is down to her last. Not only does she have little to nothing, but she is a widow and has a child to care for. In life, it normally looks easier to only be responsible for yourself when you're struggling. This would mean her burden may have been heavier than one individual could imagine. God would have to take the impossible and make it possible.

Handful of Meal

One of the things I truly admire about God is the way He moves. Not only is God saying, with Him we can't be defeated but also, 'I move on My time'. What better way to know that God is on your side than to show up when you least expect Him? So as Elijah approached the impoverished woman, there was no doubt in her mind that her life had come to an end. And out of all times, this man has asked her to prepare food for him (1 Kings 17:10-12). Instead of simply turning Elijah away, she came right out and told him her situation. 'You may need food, but we can barely feed ourselves.' She expressed how she was down to only a handful of meal. This is a moment in time, where God opened her eyes in a unique way. God didn't show up with a bag of gold and say, 'go buy the food'. He didn't show up and say, 'I'll have a job for you in the morning'. God simply said, 'Trust Me. I know you are down to your last, but trust Me.' So, although Elijah was just a man of God asking for a sacrifice, she was witnessing God being revealed. It wasn't Elijah but the act of God stepping in on her behalf.

Handful of Meal

When Elijah acknowledged her situation, he also reassured her that God would not only provide that day but for a number of days after. Could you imagine being told that the little you have will be enough to sustain you? You originally viewed it as going no further than one day but God sees beyond. God never wants the glamour and glitz. God wants the few that are faithful and committed. So as the widow rushed to do as Elijah requested, she displayed a level of faith that can only be obtained from God. What stands out in this transaction is that the woman had to first give. She couldn't only believe but also sacrifice. She had to pour into Elijah, having trust in what the man of God spoke into her life. Many of us can receive a prophetic message, but never confirm it for ourselves by believing and acting on it. Most choose to believe in their own limited sight, more than the eyes of God.

This is why I humbly call us all that do believe, God's handful of meal. An amount so small, yet spiritually powerful and unstoppable. In the human eye, we are easily outnumbered. You will find more sin and works of the devil than you will ever find the children of God. But honestly, God wants it that way. God doesn't want more sinners in the world. He simply wants to display His power. God would want nothing more than to have every last person return to their rightful place in heaven, but He also knows how we are as human beings. God knows we have been brainwashed by the extravagant portrayal of the world, and that baby steps just won't do. We read this in the battle between Moses and Pharaoh. Even though Moses did miraculous work right in front of Pharaoh's very eyes, it still wasn't enough to free God's people. In the story of David and Goliath, God could have easily brought forth someone equal to the size of Goliath or even an army, but it wouldn't have represented who God truly is and change the hearts of the lost. God wanted purpose for what He was about to do.

Now, we have our own handful of meal. We have us. Outnumbered as we are, God yet wants purpose when He does His greatest work. We are blessed to be a part of this mission. We are blessed to be what seems to be so small. You should be proud of your trials as a child of God. David never looked down on himself when he fought against the enemy. He took those stones he was given and went forth. David became another testimony in God's Book. Your life is a testimony, whether you've shared it or not. You have a purpose in life, just as the woman in 1 Kings that had gave up on life and was prepared to die. The smaller you are, the greater is our God. The devil can only attempt to look good, but his weakness is even larger than his looks. He knows he needs you and many others, in order to truly do harm in the world. The exact opposite of God. Our Creator needs no one. This is why He simply chose a handful of meal to express who He truly is.

The Struggles of the Chosen

The Struggles of the Chosen

We all know the challenges that stem from walking with Christ, but we rarely share the quiet struggles of being chosen and living in righteousness. In no way is this addressed to deter someone from choosing Jesus as their Lord and Savior but encourage them to know that the trials aren't all for nothing. In reality, the struggles are where the gifts reside. The struggles are the seeds of the future you want to plant. They become the prerequisite for the many blessings you will encounter along the way.

One of the strongest struggles in your walk is the inner voice. We all know the inner voice. The thoughts that come up at various times throughout your day. It can be thoughts that are in place to be a reminder for the day's agenda, but it will undoubtedly also include random thoughts that have little to no value. It is important to understand that every thought has a history of why it exists. There's never been a thought that wasn't linked to some area of your life. Whether it was good or bad, your history births your thoughts. This means your journey to be Christ-like will be challenged by some of the consequences of your past you don't like. The history is just that. There's no mental eraser.

Because we have history, we also have a voice that often repeats itself. It's a voice that knows very well what it is like to live according to the world's standards. It can easily retrieve what took place ten years ago, while being lackadaisical about the new understanding of God and His Word. The flesh gravitates toward what it is used to, so the voice can always bring up your previous life and behaviors. You can always remember who you were. This becomes the fight you come across spiritually. This is why Jesus informed His disciples that we must deny ourselves and take up our cross daily (Luke 9:23), because it is a daily battle. Whatever you have experienced in your life is over and done with. The only thing that matters is God, but the inner voice will attempt to go back to what is no longer there. This is what causes the struggle.

Our strength is having a knowing of both what we come up against and our true power. Thoughts are empty words. It doesn't physically exist unless we allow it. It's just like making plans for your grocery shopping, only to drive past the store and never buy anything. You may have had the grocery list on your mind but that doesn't put the groceries in your house. You still must act on the thoughts. This is the same result when it comes to having thoughts about your past. It holds no value because you can just as easily deny self and give your energy to God.

One of the greatest powers I discovered with my own inner voice is simply praising God. There's nothing more challenging for a negative spirit than trying to show itself in the midst of praise and worship. It's very easy to encounter negative thoughts in our everyday lives. You could be watching a television show or driving, and a negative thought or idea attempts to plant itself in your spirit. If your next move is to call on God and give Him praise, then you instantly override whatever tried to intervene in your life. It may not start out as an easy gesture, but everything takes work and effort. The more you practice it, the more habitual it becomes to the point it is a normal way of life. "I don't know where that came from but Hallelujah! Lord, thank You for fighting my battles. I give You praise. Glory to God!" We found a new way to praise God in our everyday lives and as Jesus said, "deny ourselves".

You're human and you face challenges and trials like any other human being that has a mind and spirit. So, you also have blemishes that you wish never happened or would simply go away. This means your thoughts are just as normal as the next person. The only way we can be different is by having those people that call out to God during their trial and those that don't have a relationship with the knowledge of turning to God. When God is not your first option, you may first attempt to fight the attack, but you can't fight anything that doesn't exist. If your thoughts were a physical person, it would make sense to fight back. You could at least attempt to defeat the opponent. Only God can handle your battles in the spirit. This is why Jesus wants to lighten your burden (Matthew 11:28-30). Those disconnected from God may not attempt to fight back but simply act on the thoughts and face the consequences. This is why any decision besides God is a lose lose situation.

The Struggles of the Chosen

As a child of God, we learn the value in our challenges. Anyone in the Holy Bible had something to gain from their trials. It was simply the understanding that what they were up against was temporal. We also grow in wisdom of our God being a just God. This means your trials not only have an expiration date but the ability to bless you as you move forward in life. The struggle will always be a blessing. The very fact that you are chosen comes with its own list of challenges, with one of them being to deny self. Overriding who the former you wants to be and accepting who God has called you to be. God never gave this responsibility to handle on your own. He knew what you would struggle with when He called on you. He also knew how much you would be blessed once you made it to the other side of the struggle and gained more understanding. The blessing is never promised to be given in a gift box. It's simply promised to bless you.

Chosen to Know God

One of the most important parts you play in the Kingdom is knowing God. This is an intimate knowing that isn't experienced by most people. There's a place within our spirit that requires us to dig deeper into this level of wisdom. When God invites you into this space, your understanding will look very different from what most display. It's never something you can brag about, but something you must nourish and share with others. It is impossible for any of us to know everything about our God, but what you do know is exactly what needs to be expressed with others. You ultimately become a key for lost souls. You're still a mortal person, but you carry a deeper understanding and the ability to teach others.

Most people with this level of awareness take on the role of a pastor or some type of teacher. With the many pastors and churches in existence, never think there's limited space for you to preach and teach God's Word. We can never have too many people that spread the Word of God. If that day ever comes, know that it will be a good thing. For now, we have more than 7 billion people in population and ample amount of opportunity to educate others about God. This is why the earth has been in existence for thousands of years and people are still being chosen to fulfill the role. And that role is simply to know God. Not being aware that there's a man in the clouds that we all must obey but truly know Him, outside of the books and stories. Discovering and acknowledging His presence in your everyday life. You begin to go beyond a limited segment of time to an all-out new thought pattern that is developing every day. A lifelong school that doesn't require a specific number of credits, but a commitment to be everything God has created you to be.

And the further you go into this life curriculum, the more you grow. The more your life begins to change to something you're not used to yet are infatuated with the entire experience. You begin to see a separation from who you once were, which may eventually lead to changes in your surroundings and the individuals you associate with. This doesn't necessarily mean you have to disown anyone because if anything, you carry a deeper concern for their well being. You begin to witness experiences in the lives of others that you once were unable to see. You begin to witness life as God's chosen. There becomes this eagerness to inform others about God and who He is to all of us, and how simply committing to Him can make a huge difference in their life. Like Jesus as He walked the earth, you may not convince everyone, but you can leave a lasting impact on the people around you.

You develop a knowing that God has always wanted you to have. He wants it to come natural to you and only flourish as you grow in life, but we seldomly know God before we know about things of the world. This is where the challenge comes in. This is where doubt, disbelief, atheism, and personal struggles come into play. This is also the importance of having a relationship with someone that knows God. Someone that not only teaches but could also speak on your behalf. In the Old Testament, this is the type of role that Moses had to fulfill. Moses would often leave the people of Israel to go and commune with God. He would later return with the message and instructions he received from God. Thanks to Jesus, no one man is required but so many of us are shallow on our understanding of God. Anyone can call out to God in the name of Jesus, but where is the relationship? What is your commitment in order to have this kind of relationship? Are you totally committed or just fell on hard times?

There's nothing difficult about knowing who God is, but we often make it hard because of how distant we are. We still want one foot in and one foot out. We want a combination of the world and God, believing we can mix it just right where 'I'm not going to hell, but I can still do my thing'. In reality, God is saying 'If you truly commit to Me, you will always experience the joys of life.' Because God already knows you. God knows you better than you know yourself. So, while you're condemning yourself for a poor decision you made, on the other hand, God already knew what was going to happen and has prepared a way out. Why not serve a God like this? Why not know a God like this? He can introduce you to things you love that you never knew existed (e.g., restaurants, recipes, relationships, businesses). God could truly blow a person's mind, but it starts with knowing Him.

The same way we can dedicate years to a school to grow in a career, we obviously have the same ability to commit to God and know Him more. And God chooses those to impart this knowledge into others that may not be able to help themselves or even know where to begin. This is why we can never have enough ministers. You can minister without a title or congregation. The very fact that you want to share the Word of God is powerful. And God has the provision to see it through. Your wisdom of God is the starting point to ignite a fire in the souls of people in countries you have yet to visit. Because regardless of how much they know, those lost have a soul that is craving for the knowledge of God. How could they not? God created them. They are not just His creation but created in His likeness. This means an individual's spirit would love nothing more than to return to its Father. "Tell me more, so that I can get closer. Share what you know about God, so that I can know God."

The Body

The Body

When you answer God's call, you become a part of 'The Body'. The bride that Jesus Christ is returning to. With all of your uniqueness and the gifts that you may have received, you fill a space within the body. What you do is instrumental in the completion of the body. Never think your gifts were only meant to be experienced on earth. A lot of people have this mindset and treat their talents as such. In reality, whatever you were given is being showcased before God. This means you should go all out in making our Father proud. We should maximize every talent that we have.

Jesus shared the importance of having gifts, when He talked about the parable involving servants and their talents (Matthew 25:14-30). We witness various amounts of talents being given. No two people were the same, so they each obviously had their own unique purpose. Regardless of the number of talents, we can agree that each servant was chosen, or they would have never received a talent. The issue resides in self worth. The servant with one talent clearly took his eyes off the source of his talent and placed his attention on what the others were blessed with. Because others had more, he saw no value in his own talent. A mistake people often make in their work for God. People often limit themselves by what others possess; never knowing that they too hold a share in the Kingdom of God. The size of your share doesn't negate the fact that you are a part of God's Kingdom and play an important role. The one talent mentioned in the parable is just as important as the other fourteen talents that were being distributed.

Our God is a just God, which means the individual given one talent will have as much of a blessing in their life as the one that receives five talents. God doesn't provide equal amounts for every individual. He provides according to your ability and desires, undoubtedly satisfying every individual completely. We saw this same perfection in the book of Exodus, involving the bread from heaven (Exodus 16:16-18). In this setting, the scriptures tell us that every man gathered the manna according to his eating. Some gathered less and some gathered more, but the amount didn't make one greater than the other. They simply gathered according to their needs. The same can easily be said for the talents. The one with five received according to his ability. The individual with one isn't less than anyone with more talents. What belittled the servant with one talent is how they viewed themself. They personally didn't believe they were enough and chose to bury their gift.

Luke 12:48 provides a great explanation of what is expected of those that receive much: "...For unto whomsoever much is given, of him shall be much required: and to whom men have committed much, of him they will ask the more." There's a price tag that comes with those gifts. God isn't just dropping presents at your doorstep. He is blessing individuals with the ability to create. From there, you must put in the work. Do you want to do five times the amount of work you already do? A lot of sacrifices are made for the many gifts you're blessed to have. Some people just can't invest that amount of time and energy, and therefore don't receive as much as someone who will. It takes nothing away from the person because they are still being blessed by God. This is why the size of your gift has no relevance in the Kingdom of God.

The Body

You can easily be judged in the world, but God is not the world, and His voice is the only voice you answer to.

In order for 'the body' to properly function, every part has to efficiently function. God knows your ability, which is why you were chosen. And if you go over and beyond with your current gifts, you can eventually be blessed with more gifts to do more for the Kingdom. What matters most is that you fulfill your assignment. You recognize the part you play in the body, regardless of the number of talents, and you utilize the talent(s) until you use them up. You leave this earth empty, so that God can know you as a good and faithful servant (Matthew 25:23). A servant He is proud to call upon. And the more you push forward to doing the Will of God, the more provision He will make available. Don't bury your gift, just because it didn't go as planned the first time, second time, third time, or even fourth time. Go back to God and find out what needs to be fixed, changed, or improved. Remember your gift and invest in it. Work it, until it begins to work. Focus on the bigger picture, the body, and the reason you are doing everything you do.

The Process

The Process

How many people talk about the process of being chosen? Not the process of studying scripture and developing a prayer life, but the process of transitioning from the person that didn't know they were chosen. The process can seem scary if you're not grounded in your knowledge of God. One of the reasons being that we must leave the person we once were. This type of process is absolutely a challenge but to an uninformed mind, it can also cause fear and doubt. This means anything you face in life is part of a process to better you. The things you must learn and the things you have to give up become a tradeoff for a life desired. Not only is it the life you want for yourself, but it is a life that God desires for you as well. This is greater than anyone could imagine because God doesn't set His desires at a mediocre level. His desires come with a purpose and intentions of leaving an impact on your life and the people you encounter.

Do you know how difficult it is to not be you? Truly ask yourself the question. The person you have spent decades and years developing, you now must walk away from. This is what it's like to discover you were chosen. You don't have to throw everything away, because a lot of it is what brought you to this point in your life. Honestly, your past becomes your testimony but now you are renewed. You speak from a better understanding and perspective about this journey of life. The 'previous you' didn't know about this, so it will often return to the things it does know. This is where the process lies. "I'm no longer the person that placed so many limitations on my life and tried to live up to the standards of others. I'm now a person with a limitless God and I embrace His standards." Depending on who you once were, change can feel like pulling teeth. The biggest issue is never knowing how rewarding it would be to 'have those teeth pulled'. This means the process could very well be painful and the average person would tell you that you have every right to give up. And no greater supporter of you giving up than yourself. How could it not be? You're the one that is enduring the pain. "It isn't worth all of this." Or even worse, "Why are all these things happening in my life?" You not only give up on the process, but you may also give up on your dreams.

The Process

There must be a process. Not you may endure some pain, but you must endure pain. It can be equated to a mother giving birth to a child. In reality, you are birthing a new individual. You are birthing a new you! This is the part of the process that makes it all make sense. You're going to eventually find yourself in a place that you thought could only be dreamed. You truly didn't put any real belief behind it, so you gave up on almost every challenging time in your life; every attempt to step into the very person you were meant to be. This is what normally happens when there's no relationship with God. Without God, the only thing you have knowledge of is the world. Whatever the world says, however the world feels, whatever the world does. Never understanding the true power of God. If every person knew the amount of power that is in only a speck of God, you would never want to be the person you once were. You would never give it a second thought. You would instead say, "Bring it on! Give me the challenges that will bring forth my future. I know that I serve a loving God that only wants what is best for my life, so there must be purpose in the pain. There must be victory in the fight." See the difference? See the amount of power that rests

The Process

behind knowledge? But this type of wisdom must be discovered. It must be in an unusual place, at an unusual time. This is what change truly is. You can't become someone different by simply being the person you have always been. You want better for yourself and better for your life, so you must become better. You must become new. You must change, and there's a process in changing.

Not only will the process develop the dreams you have for your life, but it will also help you appreciate the things you had to experience. No one sets out for pain, but we all celebrate the victory. We all know how to enjoy the fruits of our labor. As you go through the process and pain to become the new you, it is important to know our God. It is important to understand that He wouldn't allow certain things to occur in your life if it wouldn't better you. The Holy Bible doesn't tell us of a Lord that wants you to feel bad about your mistakes and failures. We learn about a God that wipes your records clean. There's more value in focusing on the future He has for you than the mess that was made in the past. If we serve a God like this and we now know this, then how could life's challenges not be for our good? Purpose. There's a purpose for the process. You could make this a mental chant for your everyday life. "There's a purpose for the process." If you want to get there from here, then you truly must go there from here. You must go through the process. You must develop the person that you desire.

It is also possible to go through pain and challenges and gain nothing from it. Gain not one red cent. And this is simply being blind of God. Not growing in your knowledge of who He is and the role He plays in your life. Then, you really are struggling in life just to be struggling because you aren't going anywhere. You are living on the 'world's time', so you can best believe that life will be hard. On God's time, there's no such thing. You will definitely have your challenges in life, but God will never allow you to have more than you can bear. He would never give you pressure just to say you were pressured. With God, experiences come into your life to bless you; regardless of how bleak they initially appear. This is why it is so important for you to know the process. Ultimately, it is required for you to know God. God doesn't sell empty

The Process

dreams. He blesses your life. To the point that you have no choice but to share your story. Tell the next person about how great God is, because it is ultimately for His good. Yes, you may live a blessed life, but you should also be telling others about their Father. A Father that has been waiting for them to call Him. Call His name with love and say, "Dad, I do love You. I do need You. I now understand Your love for me. I now understand why You waited for me. You gave me grace; even during the times I was the least deserving of Your grace. You saw me for who I really am, and this is how You choose to love me. This is why You could see the value in my process; regardless of my doubts along the way."

So, we learn to grow in God; not only know Him but also become everything He knew we could be. With greater understanding, we soon see that the process is mandatory. Without the process, we could never reach our highest potential because we would be too attached to our limited past. So, many of us must be broken to be freed from a mind of doubt and disbelief. This is an opportunity to break your lease with any limited beliefs that attempt to keep you from becoming a testament of God's goodness. Every challenge, from here on, will be a shining reflection of the blessings that God has for your life. The ability to live under His anointing and fulfill a purpose for His Kingdom. Never have the words been so important to 'trust the process'. Living for God, you can always trust the process. Regardless of how big or small it may seem; you have every reason to trust the process. Trust in the favor that God has over your life. Rarely in the world are we taught to trust in God. You may find the words on a currency, but how often are you reminded to trust God? And how often do you take those words for value? I too have had to trust in the process over my own life. It was nowhere near a 'walk in the park'. I would personally label it a walk in the wilderness because I didn't know what was going on at times. But to be entering this stage and time is remarkable. To realize it was a process to begin with, says so much about our God and how He works. Even when I eventually gave up at times, He still needed me to learn from the process. It was a class that I would have to keep taking, until I got it right. Trust in God, trust in His promises, and trust in the process.

Your Rightful Place

The same way the serpent said to Eve, 'you know the fruit of that tree is good to eat', humankind shares with one another how 'blatantly false' the Holy Bible is. Some go as far as tying the Word of God to a specific color of people. Any attempt to deter others from the true and living Word of God and our Lord Jesus Christ. This is one of the reasons I love how the scriptures never focused on a specific color of people. Our God would never have a reason to cause hate amongst His children. The only separation God is most concerned about is not having a relationship between all of humankind and Himself. This is why you often see the punishment for worships of idols and false gods being mentioned in the Holy Bible. The devil knows how powerful you are with God, so he will speak in the way that is most appropriate for you. The enemy simply wants to convince you that he is the right decision. The enemy doesn't care if it is through another religion or no religion at all, just as long as you give up on God. He just wants you to give up on your chosen place with our Lord.

I witnessed the attack firsthand. Not witnessing someone close to me being under attack but I, myself was under attack. We become unstoppable when we are in relationship with our Lord. This is why the devil hunts you down and fights for your beliefs and knowledge. Have you ever noticed how you accept a belief, make it absolute, and give your all to it? Whether the belief was established from the Holy Bible or the words of a mortal being, you made it your truth and that was it. Thankfully, some people recognize the reality of false truths and make the necessary changes; repentance and recommitting to our God. Many people digress to choosing some 'so-called beliefs' and never learning of God for themselves. Those that claim to know the Holy Bible, and deny it, gathered most of their information from word of mouth; not studying the scriptures and intimately communicating with God to have deeper understanding. It's interesting that many people accept this as accurate knowledge and not seeking the revelation for themselves; intentionally speaking to God to reveal Himself in your life and enlighten your mind. This could be compared to someone not personally knowing an individual at their workplace and as a result, choosing to believe what others have said. We see it everyday. Someone said something, sharing a half truth and creating more harm than good. When the serpent communicated with Eve, it was also half-truth. It is very true that Eve would discover the knowledge of good and evil, but it would also cause more harm than good because they would now have to fight against the knowledge of evil. Evil became an option when God never wanted His creation to have knowledge of it.

Now that evil can coexist with good in our life experience, we can be introduced to all forms of false beliefs. Good and evil are working simultaneously. This means the word; belief is just that. It can be either good or bad. A belief doesn't make it necessarily true. This is why we face many consequences throughout life because our original belief wasn't what we expected. This is why some people must pay greatly for the choices they make and their actions. They learned the flaws about their beliefs, the hard way. When it comes to religious beliefs, it can be more of a challenging journey to discover whether it's true or false. Unless a person attempts to gain a deeper understanding of who God is, they can attach to a false belief with no thought of changing. For some people, they believe they have invested too much time into their beliefs; even if there are obvious reasons to question the beliefs.

With free will, God does not force but simply desires a relationship with you. He didn't form robots, so God has no intentions of making you love Him. He will definitely make it obvious to you who He is, but it is up to us to accept God in our lives. Those that choose to ignore the signs of God have accepted whatever their fate may be. Knowing that you could have been wrong all this time is a tough fate to accept. With knowing God, there is no possibility of questioning who He is in your life. This is why those that fully commit never have a reason to think anything different. On the outside looking in, you can always choose to accept something other than God. This is what makes commitment so vital for your walk with our Lord Jesus Christ. Displaying your commitment is how God is able to reveal Himself to you. And the choice is so easy that it is readily available for all of us. It doesn't require membership or some special skill of your own.

And, it has absolutely nothing to do with religion. Religion is an organization formed by man. Even with all the followers of Jesus Christ, there are various denominations formed under the same umbrella. As long as every organization follows the Word of God, the religion is simply man's choice to have. What matters is serving God. Did you utilize the talents that were given to you? Did you share the gospel of Jesus Christ? The devil knows the simplicity of choosing Jesus Christ as your Lord, King, and Savior, and this is why he attacks in an attempt to make it difficult for you to choose. Since you only must trust, have faith in God, and follow His Word, the devil will give you multiple beliefs to choose from with the goal of making you struggle with what you believe in.

Have you ever noticed how things change for some people that stop following God? There's no longer an attack. It only makes sense because the devil no longer must fight you. Why would you have to fight unless there was something to gain? There have been many times that you were able to do a wrong thing with little to no restraint. The consequences that followed are a totally different story, but the devil definitely wasn't trying to stop you from causing more problems for yourself and the people around you. The same can be said for giving up on God. As long as you turn your back on God, the devil will be satisfied; especially if you commit to your decision and establish new beliefs. You fight to serve God because the power He gives you is too great. If a person completely converts to God's Word, they will discover abilities any regular person won't experience in a normal life without God. So instead of waiting until you have the power, the devil will start fights in any way possible. Whether it be fighting to trust God because of things being faced in the world or simply creating false truths that you may consider, the enemy just wants to deter you from continuing your walk.

The beautiful thing about following and trusting in Jesus Christ is the ability to counteract the attacks of the enemy. This means any situation or experience in your life can be followed with praise and worship of our Lord. One of the things the devil can never fight against is our Lord. The very mention of His Name causes demons to run. They cannot stay around long when the Lord is being called upon. If you are not giving in to the test and trials but instead calling on the name of the Lord, your power is embedded within you; even during the times when everything seems to be too much. With tears in your eyes, you still can't be stopped from calling on God. Even if your call is not a shout for joy but simply saying, "Though He slay me, yet will I trust in Him" (Job 13:15). Always remember who you are to God.

"I have too much invested in God. Not only the promise I made to Him, but the promise He made to me. We made an agreement for eternity. Nothing will ever be greater than this."

The Lord's Presence

It is amazing how many people are looking for gods, let alone our true God. With all the challenges faced, people in the world are feeling more and more like there is no god to turn to. The biggest problem has always been lack of understanding, which means lack of awareness. It is incredible how much God can be displayed in our everyday lives. The very reason anyone might not be seeing God at work in their life is because of no relationship. I wouldn't be able to see another human person let alone my Spiritual Father, if I had no relationship. You can know a lot about your favorite celebrity and still not truly know them, because there is no relationship. The last thing anyone would ever want is to be a stranger to God (Matthew 7:21-23). So whenever someone asks where God is, there is a great chance that God was foreign in their life to begin with. There was never time set aside to be with God. They probably spoke more to a stranger in a grocery store than they spoke to God, all week. This is why Jesus gave a warning about the consequences of not having a relationship and doing the Will of God. They will be looked upon as strangers that never had a place in heaven.

The Lord's Presence

What a devastating response to receive from such an incredible God.

So, the same way you never see a popular celebrity in your everyday life of running errands, it is quite possible to never see God; not because He's not there but simply because you don't know Him. If we used the celebrity for an example, he/she is mortal means that the celebrity exists somewhere on this earth. They physically exist and you still never see them. You can live 100 years on this earth and still never meet them, face to face. This says a lot about God. One, our Creator is spiritual. He doesn't exist in a decaying body. This means He isn't traceable to one specific area or location. Two, He is omnipresent. This means God is literally everywhere you are. You could go into a cave on a lost island, and it would change nothing about our Father. What does this say about those questioning the presence of God? There is no healthy relationship. How much time do you spend growing in God? The same way you visit a gym to build muscle or burn fat, you must purposely seek God and build that relationship.

Most people want a quick glimpse of God somewhere or somehow. If He could just flash His face one-time, this would be all they need. Maybe. The only problem with this scenario is that God does not and will not ever want a quick, brief relationship. God wants to grow in you as you grow in Him. He literally wants to build Himself within you. This is the only way you can truly know God and understand the way He moves. If someone is wanting just a little something to show that God is present, then there was never a desire to be intimate with our Lord. So, although God is all around you, it is very easy to miss Him. God is not a father of games, meaning He is not going to do the back and forth with an individual. If they haven't matured to the point of being seriously committed to anything, then they will struggle with truly knowing God because they'll keep dropping the ball. The moment they begin to get closer and things in life seem to brighten, they fall off or become impatient. God could never dedicate Himself to growing in someone that is unstable. He needs us to be dedicated to Him, for Him to be dedicated to us. Don't misunderstand this because God truly wants a

The Lord's Presence

relationship with you. It's the only reason for having mercy and grace. You could call mercy and grace, chances. And there are some people that have received chance after chance after chance after chance to get in relationship with God. That car almost hit them on the expressway, chance. They lost their job but still stayed afloat for months, chance. Their friend gave them money to buy groceries, chance. Consistently making ways in our lives because of His mercy and grace. So even when you don't see God, there is God.

One of the greatest traits that develops with your growth in God is awareness. Simply being aware that God is always right there. As you read this, He is right there. He is guiding you through life to build you up to become better and greater in your own spiritual walk. You begin to discover God in incredible ways and even the most menial ways. Something that may seem so unimportant is reassuring you that God is always there. That is one of the best ways that God works in your life, when you least expect it. Something you were unconcerned with and didn't consider, ended up giving you greater happiness and faith. If God moved in every way you expected, then there would be no need to establish great faith in Him and inherit a new level of awareness. God needs you to know that He has full control, and anything is possible in His hands. This is why when you least expect it, there He is. The perfect God that humbly gave us our Lord, to be a sacrifice for our sins. This is how you can never question the presence of our God and His love. With billions of souls calling out to Him in all parts of the world, God would love nothing more than to hear you be yet another voice that calls on His name. Because it lets God know that you still trust in Him.

"With all the people that have need of You, I trust that You will always be there when I need You. You will still protect me, like You've done so many times before. You never renege on Your Word. You are the same Lord that You were yesterday, today, and forever." (Hebrews 13:8)

Be Chosen

Be Chosen

Who wouldn't want to be chosen?

Is it safe to ask a question like that? What about: Who wouldn't want to be protected? Who wouldn't want to be at peace? Who wouldn't want to be happy? Who wouldn't want to be fed? Despite the battle that comes along with being 'picked', all of this and more is part of being chosen. And it doesn't end after 85 years. Not at all. This type of selection is made for eternity. Think about what is being said. God is choosing you for eternity. He doesn't care if you live to be 200. This doesn't change the commitment that was created. It is a marriage, not just any marriage but an eternal marriage. The book of Ephesians gives us a great display of how we are the wife of Christ (Ephesians 5:22-32). This means Jesus becomes ours, now and forever. Emphasis on forever. But would you have it any other way? You get to keep Jesus! The very Man that put it all on the line, just to save you. Crucified, just so you wouldn't go to hell!

Be Chosen

Who wouldn't want to be chosen? We channel through the books of the Holy Bible and find the most unlikely people being selected to have a place with God, displaying the fact that God loves everyone. You may not have become all that you could have been, but He still loves you. The love wasn't based on the work you did. Your work may have led to more blessings, but God loved you before you got here. That's why He created you. Could you imagine someone loving you so much that they decided to create you? You're a reflection of God's imagination. You vividly existed before the world ever saw you. You had a name, you had a personality, you had likes and dislikes, and the list goes on. God had you fully played out in His mind before you ever walked the earth. You just had to get here. You had to have certain eyes, height, and so forth. You were a choice that only our Creator could make. What more could you ask for? What better way to exist than to be smiled upon in the eyes of God? He perfectly made you, despite your differences. You may look and even feel different from others, but your worth is just as important. You have just as much of a calling as the next person.

Be Chosen

Know your value by never forgetting Who's you are. With the many lives that get cut short or never get the chance to be born, you absolutely have a purpose. You absolutely were chosen. This is why the devil wants you so badly. If I too was evil and never had the opportunity to ever be one of God's angels again, I would go out of my way to stop everyone else from being with God also. Think about it. "If I can't make it, none of you will." This is the same character that believed he was better than our God. How could you ever believe you could surpass the very God that made you? Yet, this is why we have satan as our opponent. So, since he is permanently kicked out, the devil is working overtime to keep everyone else out; especially God's chosen. The moment you hint at going in the direction of God, the devil is finding ways to disturb you, distract you, and discourage you. The only thing you need to know is that God is a warrior (Exodus 15:3). This means He is ready for battle. The only reason He allows the devil to stick around is because our God has nothing to fear. Trust and believe that if God lets you go into a storm, He can very easily bring you out. The least of His worries is expecting you to fail. What many have taught throughout history is that God had the victory before the battle started. This means by you being Team Jesus, the results of your battles are solidified. Unless God decides to change His mind, there's no way you can lose. There's no such thing as defeat.

What you must understand is that everything depends on you. Even though God wants you, Jesus wants you, the angels want you, and so on, you must make the decision. The incredible power of free will. Like most humans, we do a great job of abusing the gift of free will. And the devil knows good and well about our flaws and our free will. So, he often finds a way to tempt or at least test our blemishes in the flesh. You have Team Jesus encouraging you and helping you through, while the devil fights to entice you with everything opposite of God. And to think, with all this going on, all we must do is make a decision. We don't have to train in the gym for six months and then enter 'the ring' with gloves on. We simply say, "Devil, I'm saying no to you and yes to Jesus." We're only making a choice. Making a choice to be chosen. And as easy as it may seem, most know how challenging it actually is. Honestly, it really is only deciding, but the battle is staying laser-focused on God to continue to make the right decisions. We must walk a world engulfed with sin and find Jesus in the process. We must learn that the world is what you see, but God's is who you are. The very reason you can live and breathe is because of God. This means that God is living throughout you, whether you are doing His Will or not. You can be caught in the act of sin and still only have breath because of God's grace and mercy.

Realize that <u>you were a choice</u>, whenever you start to <u>make a choice</u>. Be the reflection of God that He always knew you were. This means imitate our God. It's obvious He believed you deserve to have life and kept you here. Wouldn't it be incredible to recognize that He deserves our praise, worship, and dedication for having us here? Our God is known as a God that never changes, never goes back on His Word, and always fulfills His promises. Can we too have this character? Can we not do the opposite of what we promised God or change it later? Let's commit to God; not like a man but like God Himself. Christ-like. We also study about a God that wants us. A God that wanted us so much that He had to let His only birthed Son be crucified to spare our eternity. Can we have this type of Passion for God and our Lord Jesus Christ? Not only have a passion but realize that your desire is not in vain. Your Father looks forward to blessing you. Taking on this type of attitude simply pulls on the heartstrings of a God that truly loves you. He loved you before you got here.

With all of this, always remember that the choices you make will go beyond a lifetime. This is forever. I ask again: Who wouldn't want to be chosen? Who wouldn't want a guarantee, not just on their life but their eternal existence? In a world of unexpectancy, we all want some sort of structure in our lives. What's more sound than a guarantee from God? Not just a god but our God, who can't lie (Numbers 23:19). You may be used to shady characteristics in the world, but now we're talking about God. We must also remember that lies are a part of evil being introduced into the world, not a part of God. So, we have a God that cannot lie and also promises to keep us covered. He is giving us a guarantee. What more could we ask for? Who wouldn't want to be chosen? The only thing that remains is our part. Do you choose God, like He chose you?

One of the unique qualities about God is that He knows how to get us right where He needs us to be. Right where we can experience Him for ourselves. It's one of the reasons God gives us all gifts, because we all can have an impact in someone's life. This is a great opportunity to recognize and remember that you too have been chosen. Even on the days it doesn't feel like it, God chose you. How powerful could that be to accept His selection, accept being God's choice? Things occur in our lives as a sign of His ever presence intervening on our behalf. Sometimes, it's a wake up call that can be shocking. Other times, it's a warm invitation to truly see what you haven't seen yet. To trust more and watch how God works. To accept your call and grow in your knowledge. To communicate more with faith that He will respond. It's times like this, where you can reflect and question whether you are responding to your call. Or, determining if you are ready to give everything to God and trust in His Will. God doesn't force you, but He will let you know that He sees you and He eagerly awaits your commitment to Him. Right now, it is very important to meditate on the fact that you are chosen. We come across information that can speak directly into our situation, and we should never forget God's grace over our lives. Everyone may not see this literature. And those that have already left earth, having no relationship with God, definitely didn't get a chance to read it. This means even the information we consume is done with purpose. You are God's and you are chosen. You are a light.

King Jesus:
"You are the light of the world. A city that is set on a hill cannot be hidden. Nor do they light a lamp and put it under a basket, but on a lampstand, and it gives light to all who are in the house. Let your light so shine before men, that they may see your good works and glorify your Father in heaven."
Matthew 5 :14 -16 NKJV

Salvation:

"In the name of our Lord Jesus Christ, God, I know I am a sinner and I know I was headed for eternal death. I ask for forgiveness of my sins and, I believe that our Lord Jesus was sacrificed for my sins that I may have eternal life. And I confess with my heart and believe that You raised our Lord Jesus from the dead. I thank You, God for salvation. In Jesus name, amen."

Made in the USA
Columbia, SC
14 July 2024